D1716078

LESBIANISM AND THE WOMEN'S MOVEMENT

Edited By

Nancy Myron & Charlotte Bunch

Diana Press

Baltimore, Md.

HQ
76
.L47

Much thanks to Coletta Reid for her very extensive help in putting this book together.

HQ
76
.L47

Library of Congress Cataloging in Publication Data

Lesbianism and the women's movement.

Bibliography: p. 104.
CONTENTS: Berson, G. The Furies.--Deevey, S. Such a nice girl.--Bunch, C. Lesbians in revolt. [etc.]
1. Lesbianism--Addresses, essays, lectures.
2. Feminism--Addresses, essays, lectures. I. Myron, Nancy, 1943- II. Bunch, Charlotte, 1944-
HQ76.L47   301.41'57   75-15637
ISBN 0-88447-006-7

Typeset, printed and bound by Diana Press, Inc., 12 West 25th St., Baltimore, Md. 21218. Single and bulk orders available by mail from Diana Press.

Contents

Lesbianism And The Women's Movement

INTRODUCTION

Four years have passed since New York Radicalesbians issued the "Woman-Identified-Woman" paper--probably the earliest statement of lesbian-feminist politics. It has been two to three years since most of these *Furies* articles were written. Yet, lesbian-feminist politics is still relatively unknown and often misunderstood among feminists. Even for lesbians, there is little collective sense of the history of our struggles from one city to another, from one year to another.

This collection of articles presents part of that history: A segment reflected through *The Furies*, a lesbian-feminist collective and newspaper in Washington DC. Written over a two-year period, the articles were authored by members of the collective and/or appeared in the newspaper. Each article discusses different questions raised by lesbian-feminist politics: heterosexual privilege, lesbian separatism, bisexuality, etc. The importance of these issues in the on-going debate over lesbianism and feminism makes this book much more than an historical relic. It is grist for that political mill.

The essence of lesbian-feminist politics is that lesbianism is political. Sounds simple. Yet, most feminists still view lesbianism as a personal decision or at best as a civil rights concern or a cultural phenomenon. Lesbianism is more than a question of civil rights and culture, although the daily discrimination against lesbians is real and its alleviation through civil libertarian reforms important. Similarly, although lesbianism is a primary force in the emergence of a dynamic women's culture, it is much more. Lesbian-feminist politics is a political critique of the institution and ideology of heterosexuality as a primary cornerstone of male supremacy. It is an extension of the analysis of sexual politics into an analysis of sex itself as an institution. It is a commitment to women as a political group which is the basis of a political/economic strategy leading to power for women, not just an "alternative community."

We are often told that "the lesbian issue" has made much progress since 1970. True, it is now on the agenda at many feminist meetings, articles use the word, lesbians don't have to hide--all the time that is--and we have more visible communities. For these small blessings, we can give thanks. However in examining the content of most discussions and articles about lesbianism, there is reason to pause in our prayers. Most positive discussions are personal, cultural, or civil rights oriented--all fine but an avoidance of the deeper political analysis. The other references to lesbianism usually boil down to an attack on our politics, whether in subtle or blatant form.

A recent experience forced me to realize that lesbian-feminism has not sunk deep roots in feminist soil. I was reading part of a thesis by a long-time feminist writer; her chapter on lesbianism ignored its political significance and focused on the personal conflicts between straights and gays. She admitted that she had not read lesbian-feminist political writings and didn't see the "lesbian issue" as

10

political. I concluded that our politics had not spread far. I asked around. The result: many feminists, even lesbians (especially those not active during the straight-gay splits of 1970-71), had little idea what lesbian-feminist politics meant.

Filling the gap in information about lesbian-feminism is one purpose of this book. But there is also a more difficult task that it addresses: answering those feminists who attack lesbian-feminists for being 1) lesbian chauvinists, 2) into oppressive sex roles, or 3) divisive to the women's movement.

In our ardor and enthusiasm for what we have discovered, lesbians may be arrogant at times. However, most "lesbian chauvinism" is a survival reaction developed to get us through the roadblocks that straight feminists erect against our ideas and experiences. The politics of the lesbian issue are still not being discussed and the label "lesbian chauvinism" is used as one excuse for this dismissal. Others say that we guilt-trip women about their personal lives, but analyzing heterosexuality necessarily raises questions about women's lives. So too does analysis of almost any issue impacting women: motherhood, marriage, etc. Are we to abandon our insights into these institutions of male supremacy in order to avoid making each other uncomfortable? Political thought and change do not develop by avoiding conflict and refusing to question what we have been taught is "natural" or "personal." What is feminism about if it is not continually challenging and changing our lives?

Some feminists divert lesbian politics by criticizing lesbian role-playing (you know, butch-femme) as anti-feminist. Most role-playing either comes out of the past oppression of lesbians who had no other models (including

11

the social necessity to pass for a straight couple) or is a result of women's efforts to get out of female passivity. The social necessity for strictly defined roles has decreased in recent years. Even so, lesbian role-playing doesn't compare to that of heterosexuals where most women *are* the 'femme' and considered "natural," not anti-feminist, even by many feminists. As such, criticism of "butch" lesbians is a criticism of any woman who steps *out* of her role. Most importantly, lesbian-feminist politics is not primarily concerned with sex-roles but with sex power; it is not the roles themselves that men and women play, but the power behind those roles that is oppressive. As we work to destroy that male power and gain female self-determination, we will create new models that replace old roles and free us to live in new ways.

Some feminists say that lesbians are "divisive to the women's movement" by demanding that every woman be a lesbian. We are less concerned with whether each woman personally becomes a lesbian than with the destruction of heterosexuality as a crucial part of male supremacy. Lesbians have been the quickest to see the challenge to heterosexuality as necessary to feminists' survival. However straight feminists are not precluded from examining and fighting against heterosexuality as an ideology and institution that oppresses us all. The problem is that few have done so. This perpetuates lesbian fears that women remaining tied to men prevents them from seeing the function of heterosexuality and acting to end it. It is not lesbians (women's ties to women), but women's ties to men, and thus men themselves, who divide women politically and personally. This is the "divisiveness" of the lesbian issue to the women's movement.

We won't get beyond this division by demanding that

lesbians retreat, politics in hand, back into the closet. We get beyond it by struggling over the institutional and ideological analysis of lesbian-feminism. We need to discover what lesbian consciousness means for any woman, just as we struggle to understand what class or race consciousness means for women of any race or class. And we must plan strategies that will destroy the political institutions that oppress us.

Most lesbian-feminists have difficulty imagining why a woman with lesbian consciousness would choose a man and cut herself off from the strength of women loving women. Nevertheless, we can make allies on the basis of political consciousness/action with all feminists who fight heterosexuality. Similarly straight feminists must stop hiding behind the excuses that lesbians are chauvinist or divisive and instead examine the political basis of lesbian-feminism. Doing so, we can more effectively fight heterosexuality as an institution that hinders the development of a strong women's community and female power.

Some new bonds are beginning to emerge between lesbians and single women. We share a common economic and psychological reality: we are solely responsible for our lives--all of our lifetime. We have rejected ownership by men and with it, economic support. We face survival issues without heterosexual cushions and come closer to the reality always faced by lower class women, whether lesbian or heterosexual. We must provide for ourselves, our children, and each other--economically, emotionally, and if we organize, politically. This economic and psychological reality develops more strength and spirit in individual women. Collectively, this strength can be transformed into the power and soul of a forceful feminist movement.

THE FURIES

Ginny Berson

The story of the Furies is the story of strong, powerful women, the 'Angry Ones', the avengers of matricide, the protectors of women. Three Greek Goddesses, they were described (by men) as having snakes for hair, bloodshot eyes, and bats' wings; like Lesbians today, they were cursed and feared. They were born when Heaven (the male symbol) was castrated by his son at the urging of Earth (the female symbol). The blood from the wound fell on Earth and fertilized her, and the Furies were born. Their names were Alecto (Never-ceasing), Tisiphone (Avenger of Blood), and Magaera (Grudger). Once extremely powerful, they represented the supremacy of women and the primacy of mother right.

Their most famous exploit (famous because in it they lost much of their power) involved Orestes in the last epi-

15

sode connected with the cycle of the Trojan War. Orestes, acting on the orders of the Sun God Apollo, killed his mother Clytemnestra, because she had killed his father. Clytemnestra had killed the father because he had sacrificed their daughter Iphigenia, in order to get favorable winds so his fleet could sail to Troy. The Furies tormented Orestes: they literally drove him crazy, putting him under a spell where for days he could not eat or wash his blood-stained hands. He bit off his finger to try to appease them, but to no avail. Finally, in desperation, Orestes went before the court of Athena to plead his case.

The point at issue was whether matricide was justifiable to avenge your father's murder, or in other words, whether men or women were to dominate. Apollo defended Orestes and totally denied the importance of motherhood, claiming that women were no more than sperm receptacles for men, and that the father was the only parent worthy of the name. One might have thought that Athena, Goddess of Wisdom, would have condemned Orestes, but Athena was the creation of the male God, Zeus, sprung full-grown from his head, the first token woman. Athena decided for Orestes. Some mythologists say that Zeus, Athena, and Apollo had conspired from the beginning, ordering Orestes to kill his mother in order to put an end, once and for all, to the religious belief that motherhood was more divine than fatherhood. In any case, that was the result.

The Furies were, of course, furious, and threatened to lay waste the city of Athens. But Athena had a direct line to Zeus, King of the Gods; she told the Furies to accept the new male supremacist order or lose everything. Some of the Furies and their followers relented, the rest pursued Orestes until his death.

We call our paper *The Furies* because we are also angry. We are angry because we are oppressed by male supremacy. We have been fucked over all our lives by a system which is based on the domination of men over women, which defines male as good and female as only as good as the man you are with. It is a system in which heterosexuality is rigidly enforced and Lesbianism rigidly suppressed. It is a system which has further divided us by class, race, and nationality.

We are working to change this system which has kept us separate and powerless for so long. We are a collective of twelve Lesbians living and working in Washington, D.C. We are rural and urban; from the Southwest, Midwest, South and Northeast. Our ages range from 18 to 28. We are high school drop-outs and Ph.D. candidates. We are lower class, middle and upper-middle class. We are white. Some of us have been Lesbians for twelve years, others for ten months. We are committed to ending all oppressions by attacking their roots--male supremacy.

We believe *The Furies* will make important contributions to the growing movement to destroy sexism. As a collective, in addition to outside projects, we are spending much time building an ideology which is the basis for action. For too long, women in the Movement have fallen prey to the very male propaganda they seek to refute. They have rejected thought, building an ideology, and all intellectual activity as the realm of men, and tried to build a politics based only on feelings--the area traditionally left to women. The philosophy has been, "If it feels good, it's O.K. If not, forget it." But that is like saying that strength, which is a "male" characteristic, should be left to men, and women should embrace weakness. Most straight women, to say nothing of men, feel afraid or contemptuous of Lesbians. That fear and contempt is similar to the feelings middle class whites have towards Blacks or lower class people. These feelings are the result of our socialization and are hardly worth glorifying. This is not to say that feelings are irrelevant, only that they are derived from our experience which is limited by our class, race, etc. Furthermore, feelings are too often used to excuse inaction and inability to change.

A political movement cannot advance without systematic thought and practical organization. The haphazard, non-strategic, zig-zag tactics of the straight women's movement, the male left, and many other so-called revolutionary groups have led only to frustration and dissolution. We do not want to make those same mistakes; our ideology forms the basis for developing long-range strategies and short-term tactics, projects, and actions.

The base of our ideological thought is: Sexism is the root of all other oppressions, and Lesbian and woman oppression will not end by smashing capitalism, racism, and imperialism. Lesbianism is not a matter of sexual preference, but rather one of political choice which every woman must make if she is to become woman-identified and thereby end male supremacy. Lesbians, as outcasts from every culture but their own have the most to gain by ending class, race, and national supremacy within their own ranks. Lesbians must get out of the straight women's movement and form their own movement in order to be taken seriously, to stop straight women from oppressing us, and to force straight women to deal with their own Lesbianism. Lesbians cannot develop a common politics with women who do not accept Lesbianism as a political issue.

In *The Furies* we will be dealing with these issues

18

and sharing our thoughts with you. We want to build a movement in this country and in the world which can effectively stop the violent, sick, oppressive acts of male supremacy. We want to build a movement which makes all people free.

For the Chinese women whose feet were bound and crippled; for the Ibibos of Africa whose clitori were mutilated; for every woman who has ever been raped, physically, economically, psychologically, we take the name of *The Furies*, Goddesses of Vengeance and protectors of women.

The Furies, January 1972

SUCH A
NICE GIRL

Sharon Deevey

In February 1969 I joined a Women's Liberation study group in Washington, D.C. As we read Engels' *Origin of the Family* I knew I had found other women who shared my anger, frustration, and hopes. I stopped trying to organize "radical teachers" and quit my job as an elementary school teacher to work full time in the women's movement.

Between September 1969 and the spring of 1970, Women's Liberation reached its first peak in energy, participation, and media coverage. Hundreds of women came week after week to our free university course. We opened an office and were flooded with mail, phone calls, and "new" women. Our projects and actions on daycare, abortion, the pill, and the war kept us out all day and up all night. Our enthusiasm, which we called female life-force, infected the left movement in the city, including husbands and boyfriends of many W.L. women. At softball games, parties, and communal suppers, women challenged men about their chauvinism in a mock-serious way which did not threaten the growing sense of community. My husband paid our bills, washed the dishes half the time, and wanted to know everything that happened at every women's meeting.

By the spring of 1970 we had developed a descriptive analysis of the oppression of white, middle-class American wives and mothers, which most of us were. We practiced a fly-swatter, help-your-sister approach to ending the oppresion of women. We were confused by guilt feelings about black, poor, and third world women. Where could we go from there?

Several women who had been leaders in W.L. got together to form a working collective. We knew we were beginning to flounder. We had ideas but no overall direction and less energy. We rejected leadership but were still leaders. We prided ourselves that Washington avoided factionalism, and tried to figure out an individual explanation every time some one dropped out of the group instead of understanding the political reasons why people did not stay. Most of all we believed "sisterhood is powerful" and that an analysis and strategy for our liberation would simply come out of our good vibes and our renewed seriousness.

In the meantime I had fallen in love with Joan and was scared shitless that I would be kicked out of Women's Liberation if anyone found out. At meetings in the W.L. office, women protested loudly whenever the media or men denounced W.L. as a "bunch of lesbians". Each time I looked at the floor and waited for them to go home so Joan and I could lock the door and make love.

Gradually we told our friends, and while we were both

relating to my husband, no one was very upset. Bisexuality was seen as progressive. The real threat, and the real contradictions in the women's movement, only became clear when Joan and I ended our attempts to relate to my husband.

I had never questioned or thought of heterosexuality as an institution. Now, I began to understand that everything I had thought was "natural" was a vicious lie maintained to keep women down. I was as disoriented as my friends were threatened. I was very conscious of changing. A crucial part of my conditioning as a woman was to be passive, to let things happen to me. Now I was deciding to be different and make things happen. My friends, and their husbands, explained to each other that I had been stolen from my husband by a man-hating lesbian. Their hatred of Joan as a "real" lesbian only emphasized their need to continue seeing me as a passive, duped, non-threatening "real woman".

As I experienced the combined exhiliration of loving a woman and knowing I could change, I thought all women would come out, change and be as happy as I was. Most of my friends didn't change and come out; I gradually emerged from my "new gay" euphoria to find myself in an alien world. I thought I had been fighting pig America before, but because of my class, race and heterosexual privilege, I had fought as a rebel, not as a reject. Everything around me was, and of course, always had been, heterosexual--men and women together, and men most important. Books, movies, people in the streets, my family, my friends, and especially Women's Liberation: birth control, bad fucks, and abortions! I had belatedly discovered lesbian oppression. I was a *queer* and I was going to have to fight in order to survive *myself*. I had taught myself to shoplift to "prac-

23

tice" for the revolution, but now as a lesbian I had to lie every day to survive in the Man's world.

Much of my new oppression as a lesbian was coming from my heterosexual friends--the women I had worked with and loved in W.L. I was a "nice" lesbian who explained to them over and over, as many times as they asked, why I was a lesbian and how I was oppressed. At first I did not push anyone to come out, even as I began to see that lesbianism is a political choice. I kept reassuring them and myself, that we could continue to work together.

I wasted energy and emotion on them too long. They had *said* "women should love women--men keep women apart--women together can change the world". Because they wouldn't or couldn't live up to those ideas, they are traitors to their own vision. They have been bought off by the privilege and security they get from men. They have betrayed women, especially themselves. A women's revolution can be made by women only who give their full energy and love to each other, that is, by lesbians.

Only after I had kicked out my husband did I see how much heterosexuality had blocked my real understanding of men and male supremacy. I could let myself remember the disgust I had initially felt about fucking. I realized that *every* fuck is a rape even if it feels nice because every man has power and privilege over women, whether he uses it blatantly or subtly. My "liberated" husband kept me down not by violence but by making me feel guilty. He wanted me to be a strong woman as long as my main worries were about his feelings, problems, and "oppression". In a conversation, when the guilt tactic no longer worked on me, he sat in disbelief, and I saw him consider whether to fall back on the male power which he had always had in reserve. As a heterosexual I had always had to double-

24

think, "well, my man is an exception" every time I got close to the truth, that male supremacy is the source of all oppression, and that *every* man benefits from it. As a lesbian I have begun to experience how it will be fundamentally different as women begin to build our own world. As long as I gave energies to my man, I had not experienced that tremendous difference.

When I first came out I thought of myself as better than "old" lesbians. I believed in my "superior women's consciousness" and my "revolutionary life-style." I was afraid of bar lesbians and offended by "sexist" camp humor. In fact I looked at lesbians with all the prejudice and fear I had learned as a heterosexual. I still wanted to be "normal" and to keep my heterosexual privileges. As I saw through the perversion of *heterosexuality* and experienced the shit that came down from my straight friends, my identification as a lesbian--*a man-hating dyke*--became clear to me. I cut my hair as a symbolic cut with my past, and because I wanted to look like a "real" lesbian. The bar which had frightened me at first became my refuge too.

I gave up some of my privilege by becoming a dyke. But I am only now understanding some of the rest of my privilege and how to change it. About a year ago I joined a lesbian collective that lived together one painful week and broke up, largely because several of us had not dealt with our class privilege. I had thought that eight gay women living together would be heaven after the isolation of being the only lesbians in Women's Liberation. But I was so consumed by what I thought was "revolutionary"--communal everything, non-monogamy, dope--that I resisted any criticism about my class behavior. Class had been mentioned but not understood in the heterosexual women's movement, because we spent all our time dealing with

25

men instead of with each other, and because the organization was started and controlled by middle class white women who couldn't or wouldn't see that our class behavior was the cause of many of the problems that so distressed us.

There are many ways in which I have not changed enough about class. Some of them I understand and just have to *do* something about. I know there is a lot I don't understand yet about class, and I have hardly begun to deal with race. I did change from a heterosexual to a lesbian, and from heterosexual consciousness to lesbian consciousness. I am frustrated and angry at women who cling to their privilege and refuse to make that change. Working class women are just as angry at me, for the same good reason. The revolution means change...women changing themselves...women changing the world. There is no middle ground and no individual solution. If you, or I, choose not to change, we choose against a women's revolution and against ourselves.

The Furies, January 1972

LESBIANS IN REVOLT

Charlotte Bunch

The development of Lesbian-Feminist politics as the basis for the liberation of women is our top priority; this article outlines our present ideas. In our society which defines all people and institutions for the benefit of the rich, white male, the Lesbian is in revolt. In revolt because she defines herself in terms of women and rejects the male definitions of how she should feel, act, look, and live. To be a Lesbian is to love oneself, woman, in a culture that denegrates and despises women. The Lesbian rejects male sexual/political domination; she defies his world, his social organization, his ideology, and his definition of her as inferior. Lesbianism puts women first while the society declares the male supreme. Lesbianism threatens male supremacy at its core. When politically conscious and organized, it is central to destroying our sexist, racist, capitalist, imperialist system.

29

Lesbianism is a Political Choice

Male society defines Lesbianism as a sexual act, which reflects men's limited view of women: they think of us only in terms of sex. They also say Lesbians are not real women, so a real woman is one who gets fucked by men. We say that a Lesbian is a woman whose sense of self and energies, including sexual energies, center around women--she is woman identified. The woman-identified-woman commits herself to other women for political, emotional, physical, and economic support. Women are important to her. She is important to herself. Our society demands that commitment from women be reserved for men.

The Lesbian, woman-identified-woman, commits herself to women not only as an alternative to oppressive male/female relationships but primarily because she *loves* women. Whether consciously or not, by her actions, the Lesbian has recognized that giving support and love to men over women perpetuates the system that oppresses her. If women do not make a commitment to each other, which includes sexual love we deny ourselves the love and value traditionally given to men. We accept our second class status. When women do give primary energies to other women, then it is possible to concentrate fully on building a movement for our liberation.

Woman-identified Lesbianism is, then, more than a sexual preference, it is a political choice. It is political because relationships between men and women are essentially political, they involve power and dominance. Since the Lesbian actively rejects that relationship and chooses women, she defies the established political system.

Lesbianism, By Itself, Is Not Enough

Of course, not all Lesbians are consciously woman-iden-tified, nor are all committed to finding common solutions to the oppression they suffer as women and Lesbians. Being a Lesbian is part of challenging male supremacy, but not the end. For the Lesbian or heterosexual woman, there is no individual solution to oppression.

The Lesbian may think that she is free since she escapes the personal oppression of the individual male/female relationship. But to the society she is still a woman, or worse, a visible Lesbian. On the street, at the job, in the schools, she is treated as an inferior and is at the mercy of men's power and whims. (I've never heard of a rapist who stopped because his victim was a Lesbian). This society hates women who love women, and so, the Lesbian, who escapes male dominance in her private home, receives it doubly at the hands of male society; she is harrassed, outcast, and shuttled to the bottom. Lesbians must become feminists and fight against woman oppression, just as feminists must become Lesbians if they hope to end male supremacy.

U.S. society encourages individual solutions, apolitical attitudes, and reformism to keep us from political revolt and out of power. Men who rule, and male leftists who seek to rule, try to depoliticize sex and the relations between men and women in order to prevent us from acting to end our oppression and challenging their power. As the question of homosexuality has become public, reformists define it as a private question of who you sleep with in order to sidetrack our understanding of the politics of sex. For the Lesbian-Feminist, it is not private; it is a political matter of oppression, domination, and power. Reformists offer solutions which make no basic changes in the system that oppresses us, solutions which keep power in the hands of the oppressor. The only way oppressed people end their oppression is by seizing power: People whose rule depends on the subordination of others do not voluntarily stop oppressing others. Our subordination is the basis of male power.

Sexism Is the Root of All Oppression

The first division of labor, in pre-history, was based on sex: men hunted, women built the villages, took care of children, and farmed. Women collectively controlled the land, language, culture, and the communities. Men were able to conquer women with the weapons that they developed for hunting when it became clear that women were leading a more stable, peaceful, and desirable existence. We do not know exactly how this conquest took place, but it is clear that the original imperialism was male over female: the male claiming the female body and her service as his territory (or property).

Having secured the domination of women, men continued this pattern of suppressing people, now on the basis of tribe, race, and class. Although there have been numerous battles over class, race, and nation during the past 3000 years, none has brought the liberation of women. While these other forms of oppression must be ended, there is no reason to believe that our liberation will come with the smashing of capitalism, racism, or imperialism today. Women will be free only when we concentrate on fighting male supremacy.

Our war against male supremacy does, however, involve

attacking the latter day dominations based on class, race, and nation. As Lesbians who are outcasts from every group, it would be suicidal to perpetuate these man-made divisions among ourselves. We have no heterosexual privileges, and when we publicly assert our Lesbianism, those of us who had them lose many of our class and race privileges. Most of our privileges as women are granted to us by our relationships to men (fathers, husbands, boyfriends) whom we now reject. This does not mean that there is no racism or class chauvinism within us, but we must destroy these divisive remnants of privileged behavior among ourselves as the first step toward their destruction in the society. Race, class, and national oppressions come from men, serve ruling class white men's interests, and have no place in a woman-identified revolution.

Title

Lesbianism is the Basic Threat to Male Supremacy

Lesbianism is a threat to the ideological, political, personal, and economic basis of male supremacy. The Lesbian threatens the ideology of male supremacy by destroying the lie about female inferiority, weakness, passivity, and by denying women's 'innate' need for men. Lesbians literally do not need men (even for procreation if the science of cloning is developed).

The Lesbian's independence and refusal to support one man undermines the personal power that men exercise over women. Our rejection of heterosexual sex challenges male domination in its most individual and common form. We offer all women something better than submission to personal oppression. We offer the beginning of the end of collective and individual male supremacy. Since men of all races and classes depend on female support and sub-

33

mission for practical tasks and feeling superior, our refusal to submit will force some to examine their sexist behavior, to break down their own destructive privileges over other humans, and to fight against those privileges in other men. They will have to build new selves that do not depend on oppressing women and learn to live in social structures that do not give them power over anyone.

Heterosexuality separates women from each other; it makes women define themselves through men; it forces women to compete against each other for men and the privilege which comes through men and their social standing. Heterosexual society offers women a few privileges as compensation if they give up their freedom: for example, mothers are respected and 'honored', wives or lovers are socially accepted and given some economic and emotional security, a woman gets physical protection on the street when she stays with her man, etc. The privileges give heterosexual women a personal and political stake in maintaining the status quo.

The Lesbian receives none of these heterosexual privileges or compensations since she does not accept the male demands on her. She has little vested interest in maintaining the present political system since all of its institutions--church, state, media, health, schools--work to keep her down. If she understands her oppression, she has nothing to gain by supporting white rich male America and much to gain from fighting to change it. She is less prone to accept reformist solutions to women's oppression.

Economics is a crucial part of woman oppression, but our analysis of the relationship between capitalism and sexism is not complete. We know that Marxist economic theory does not sufficiently consider the role of women or

Lesbians, and we are presently working on this area.

However, as a beginning, some of the ways that Lesbians threaten the economic system are clear: In this country, women work for men in order to survive, on the job and in the home. The Lesbian rejects this division of labor at its roots; she refuses to be a man's property, to submit to the unpaid labor system of housework and childcare. She rejects the nuclear family as the basic unit of production and consumption in capitalist society.

The Lesbian is also a threat on the job because she is not the passive/part-time woman worker that capitalism counts on to do boring work and be part of a surplus labor pool. Her identity and economic support do not come through men, so her job is crucial and she cares about job conditions, wages, promotion, and status. Capitalism cannot absorb large numbers of women demanding stable employment, decent salaries, and refusing to accept their traditional job exploitation. We do not understand yet the total effect that this increased job dissatisfaction will have. It is, however, clear that as women become more intent upon taking control of their lives, they will seek more control over their jobs, thus increasing the strains on capitalism and enhancing the power of women to change the economic system.

Lesbians Must Form our own Movement
To Fight Male Supremacy

Feminist-Lesbianism, as the most basic threat to male supremacy, picks up part of the Women's Liberation analysis of sexism and gives it force and direction. Women's Liberation lacks direction now because it has failed to understand the importance of heterosexuality in maintaining male supremacy and because it has failed to face class and race as real differences in women's behavior and political needs. As long as straight women see Lesbianism as a bedroom issue, they hold back the development of politics and strategies which would put an end to male supremacy and they give men an excuse for not dealing with their sexism.

Being a Lesbian means ending identification with, allegiance to, dependence on, and support of heterosexuality. It means ending your personal stake in the male world so that you join women, individually and collectively, in the struggle to end your oppression. Lesbianism is the key to liberation and only women who cut their ties to male privilege can be trusted to remain serious in the struggle against male dominance. Those who remain tied to men, individually or in political theory, cannot always put women first. It is not that heterosexual women are evil or do not care about women. It is because the very essense, definition, and nature of heterosexuality is men first. Every woman has experienced that desolation when her sister puts her man first in the final crunch: heterosexuality demands that she do so. As long as women still benefit from heterosexuality, receive its privileges and security, they will at some point have to betray their sisters, especially Lesbian sisters who do not recieve those benefits.

Women in women's liberation have understood the importance of having meetings and other events for women only. It has been clear that dealing with men divides us and saps our energies and that it is not the job of the oppressed to explain our oppression to the oppressor. Women also have seen that collectively, men will not deal with their sexism until they are forced to do so. Yet, many of these same women continue to have primary relationships with men individually and do not understand why Lesbians find this oppressive. Lesbians cannot grow politically or personally in a situation which denies the basis of our politics: that Lesbianism is political, that heterosexuality is crucial to maintaining male supremacy.

Lesbians must form our own political movement in order to grow. Changes which will have more than token effects on our lives will be led by woman-identified Lesbians who understand the nature of our oppression and are therefore in a position to end it.

The Furies, January 1972

TAKING
THE BULLSHIT
BY THE HORNS

Barbara Solomon

I've heard a lot of women criticize *The Furies* article, "Lesbians In Revolt." Their criticism has not gone any further than to label the article elitist and arrogant. Such criticism does not deal with the political differences these women feel with the article. All it says is, "Reading this demanded a political response from me that was too threatening." This kind of thinking has been generated by the straight women's liberation movement which as *The Furies* introduction pointed out has defined political analysis as men's realm and left women acting on an emotional level. Since thinking about the article won't feel good for a lot of women, it's easier for them to call it arrogant and ignore what it says.

Some Lesbians I know who read the article said, "There's no difference between straight and gay," or "People need other people to love them and if a woman can get love from a man, that's cool," and "I don't like to sleep with men, but they *are* going to be around after the revolution, and I could care less if another woman is sleeping with a man."

These Lesbians probably crystallized their politics in the Gay Liberation Movement, which was an appendage of the New Left and which was run by men. Gay Liberation defined the enemy of gayness as public opinion that gay is perverted, and acted to disprove that notion. There were two standard arguments used. The first said that straight people need to loosen up and let everybody do their own thing. This argument equates Lesbian lifestyle and sexuality with gay men's, when in fact there are crucial differences.

The second argument said, "Do what feels good. Sex is groovy. Gay is just as good as straight. I don't care what you do in bed, so you shouldn't care what I do in bed." This argument assumes that Lesbians have the same lifestyle and sexuality as straight women. But we don't ---straight women choose to love and fuck men. Lesbians have commitments to women.

Lesbians are not born. We have made a conscious choice to be Lesbians. We have rejected all that is traditonal and accepted, and committed ourselves to a lifestyle that everybody---straight men, straight women, gay men---criticizes. So most of us question this choice over and over again, and we are still Lesbians. Therefore every Lesbian knows in her gut that what we do is not the same as gay men---they oppress us too---and what we do is not the same as what straight women do. If it were, we wouldn't have chosen to be Lesbians in the first place.

Implicit Feminist Political Principle

Implicit in the Lesbian lifestyle is a Feminist political principle. That does not mean that all Lesbians are Feminists. It just means that we have chosen living with and loving women, that we have rejected living with and loving men. Since straight women get some compensations for being straight which we have forfeited, then Lesbianism further says that we get something better from women than we do from men, or that we get something worse by relating to men that we do not get relating to women. Or both.

We live in a male supremacist shitpile. At its most basic level this shitpile is upheld by fucking, marriage and breeding. Straight women serve this system by serving their men. Lesbians reject it by saying we won't fuck, we won't marry, we won't breed and we'll damn well do as we please.

And we are oppressed for it. Our biggest oppression is *not* that everybody thinks we're perverted. Women think we're perverted because women have been handed a whole set of morals. But men have never given a shit about morals and they could care less about perversion. Men tell women that we're perverted because men know that what we're doing is going to take their power away from them right where it hurts. Men see us saying that we don't want men in our beds and we don't want men in our houses and we don't want men in our bars. And they know that it is a very short step from there for us to say that we don't want men living on the street, we don't

41

want men in our government, and in fact we would be 100% better off if we just didn't have to deal with men at all.

They don't think there is anything perverted about that. They recognize it for what it is and oppress us, stick us away in ghettoes and tell their wives and daughters that we're disgusting. Now any woman who gets raped by her husband every day, who has to live under his psychological and economic control, and had to grovel before him and lap up the shit that he ladles all over her knows that *that* is pretty damn disgusting and perverted. She is only too happy to hear that there is somebody lower on the pecking order than herself.

Heterosexuality Insures Male Supremacy

Heterosexuality insures male supremacy. To say that "Everybody needs love and I could care less if a woman is fucking a man" is to say "Any oppressed person needs some payoff to make them preserve their oppression. I could care less if a woman is oppressed, and I could care less if that oppression makes her gang up with that pig to fuck me over." The only Lesbians who could say this are Lesbians with a bigger stake in their own oppression than in our liberation; i.e., Lesbians who use their class and race privileges, Lesbians in the nouveau chic of the New Left, etc.

Lesbians have the potential to smash male supremacy. Straight women do not, because they are living its perpetration. *The Furies* article on Roxanne Dunbar summed this up very accurately, "*I know full well there are women who physically love other women who could sell us out as quickly as any man or straight woman. Some of them* are racist, class snobs and outright reactionaries. By the same token, all working class people are not committed to the destruction of capitalism. There are plenty of racists and fascists among the workers. The essential point is that workers carry the greatest threat to capitalism if organized just as Lesbians carry the greatest threat to male supremacy if organized."

We can extend this analysis further. The middle class depends on capitalism for its privileges, although some middle class people feel oppressed by capitalism and are organizing. Because their interests lie with their oppressors', they are capable of organizing as a power bloc to minimize their petty oppressions at the expense of the working class and expand their privileges.

And so with women. Straight women are oppressed by men, but their lifestyle and privileges are nevertheless dependent upon their individual relationships with men. When they organize, they seek to minimize that oppression at the expense of other women, and grab more privileges.

"Sisterhood Is Groovy"

Straight women's liberation started the myth that sisterhood is groovy. Sisterhood is so groovy that if put to use by straight, racist, classist women it can make it easier and better for them to maintain their lackey relationships with the men who oppress us all.

The Women's Liberation movement has completely avoided making any kind of ideology about our oppression because that would expose the contradiction they are living in. So they left politics to the big, strong men and developed a philosophy of being "sensitive." They have

43

expressed their sisterly feelings by making us slaves for their personal liberation. They say that all women are sisters despite sexuality, race or class. Then they organize us and put our sisterhood to work for reforms that only benefit white, middle class, straight women.

The abortion movement is a good example of what happens when privileged people organize. Abortion is a reform measure. Its analysis is good when it says that women should seize control of their own bodies, but it patently ignores the contradiction that women will not have control of their own bodies if they keep on voluntarily giving them to men, Abortion, then, does not threaten male supremacy. It assumes that women are going to keep on fucking and breeding and makes it easier for some women to lick up to men.

Straight women tried to rally us all together under the "Sisterhood is groovy" banner to win abortions. Straight privileged women said that sex, class or race issues would be divisive and would keep us from winning. Then they proceeded to use us to win abortions that are totally irrelevant to Lesbians, can be used as genocide against Third World women, and are too expensive for poor women to afford. Oh, Sisterhood is so groovy.

The biggest rip-off of the Sisterhood is groovy line is that it says women should get together and get stronger and take care of each other's needs independently. This is great. But if some of those women are depending on men in their personal lives, then they are going to depend on women to fill the needs that those men cause them. Any woman who expects other women to fill her needs has a responsibility to minimize those needs by immediately eliminating any of the needs caused by living with or sucking up to an oppressor.

44

Straight Women Want Payoffs

Straight women don't want us to fight with men--they just want pay-offs from men *and* women. Since women have been defined as always-giving, women who define themselves through women should always give--to them. They don't think that they are important enough to deserve anything from men, but because they're "real women" who get fucked by men, they think they deserve something from us. The reason they would rather exhaust our energy than join us in ripping off what we need from men is very simple: The man who's got it is giving her some crumbs. She's been conditioned to think that she doesn't deserve anything more than the crumbs, so if we start taking whole pieces of the pie, it might make less crumbs for her. On the other hand, if she stays in middle-of-the-road straight women's liberation, she can play us off against her man and get the best of both worlds. He's going to have to start behaving--washing the dishes, taking care of the kids, and being a good lay--or she might leave him and become a man-hating dyke. (He knows her friends are subverting her.) Meanwhile, we've got to prove to her that we're better than men--if we *also* wash her dishes, take care of the kids, help her try to change her old man and show him the light, hold her hand when he fucks her over but don't alienate her or hurt her feelings by telling her to leave him, and to top it all off, if we seem like desirable sex objects--then she might leave him to become a man-hating dyke, and reward us with her love. (If she changes her mind later she can always say that we subverted her.)

Every Lesbian knows through personal experience how

straight women sell us out. Each of us at some time has been infatuated with a straight woman and we compromised ourselves, grovelled to be good to her and tried to prove to her that we were better than men, all in hopes that she would love us. Meanwhile she feminized us--kept us passive in intimidation, ashamed of ourselves, pretty, dangling, kissing up to her and very, very vulnerable. Whenever we were hurt she was too busy with the men in her life to help us out. If any man found her out, she told him that we were dirty and disgusting and had done horrible things to her. Then he "saved" her and she paid him back by giving him a lifetime of services and free fucks. She had to betray us, because her interests were hanging on some man's prick.

"Lesbians in Revolt" does not say that all Lesbians are necessarily feminists. It says that we are a very big threat to male supremacy, and if we're together with each other, we can bring that beast down. And it says that for sure any woman relating to a man cannot be a feminist. Women who give love and energy to men rather than women obviously think men are better than women. Therefore they will wish to remain in a society that says men are better than women, and they'll join their boyfriends in trying to do us in.

It's really sad that every man holds a woman in front of him to cushion reality and be his shield. Some women are so well trained that they'll run right out on their own to protect him and bare their own necks instead. When we pick a fight with a man, it seems like we can't even get close enough to kick unless we want to kick all those women out of the way first. That's why straight women's liberation tells us Sisterhood is so groovy. We've been kept from fighting our oppression because our enemies are just crawling all over with women who want to protect them, and fighting with women is a no-no.

Well, I'm not going to try to take on all those woman if I don't have to. I am just stating that I personally am going to keep my distance from men and straight women. Maybe we can run around behind and stab that pig in the back. Any woman hanging out in front to protect him would then have the choice of joining us or letting him fall on top of her.

The Furies, March-April, 1972

LESBIANS AND THE CLASS POSITION OF WOMEN

Margaret Small

I would like to talk about the class position of women--in what way women are, by virtue of being women, a class that is exploited by men. I want to talk about the basis of that exploitation, the role of heterosexual ideology in maintaining it and the power of lesbians for breaking it.

Marxist ideology begins with the assumption that the material conditions of life determine all other structures. By material conditions Marx means our efforts at producing those things which meet our basic needs. How we get those things--food, clothing, shelter--determines how we view the world. Psychology, religion, morals, etc. are all part of a super-structure growing out of and reflecting the basic economic facts of our lives. In other words, if we were serfs in a feudal society--bound to the land, owing allegiance to a lord, etc.--we would have a different psychology, a different religion, a different way of looking at the world than if we were wage-laborers in a corporate capitalist society. The

"Lesbians and the Class Position of Women" is a condensed and edited text of a speech by Margaret Small given at the Institute for Policy Studies on behalf of *The Furies.*

49

circumstances and structures through which we produce, maintain and continue our livelihood determine the rest of our life.

Marx saw external production--working in the wage economy--as *the* material condition. That formulation takes for granted all the work that women do--the maintenance and production of daily life itself. Marxist analysis assumes rather than analyzes the most basic production and reproduction. Thus, Marxists have no way of analyzing women's class position. Their only solution is to try and fit women into their analysis of external production--the situation of men.

There are three elements that define the oppression of women--reproduction, production (domestic labor), and sexuality. These material conditions are interrelated historically and today. Each has its own dynamic, each comes out of a particular material situation, and each is an actual objective condition.

Material Basis of Women's Oppression

Women's oppression is based in the fact that she reproduces the species. The relationship of men to reproduction is defined by a single act of fucking at the moment of impregnation and ends at that point. Women's responsibility for the reproduction of the species is the basis for the sexual division of labor.

In early agricultural societies as groups settled in particular geographical locations, women reproduced the children, cared for the children, and were responsible for the basic development of food and tools. Prior to highly-centralized patriarchal societies, women had a fairly independent relationship to the means of production. They had access to

50

materials, their own land, their own food supplies and were responsible for meeting the needs of the population. Women did whatever was necessary for the survival of themselves and their children: they developed agriculture, crafts, language, etc. Men were fairly peripheral; they were not the core holding the social organization together.

As women developed technology, they created a significant surplus--more than enough for the actual material needs of life. At that point men began to appropriate the surplus. Women then not only met their own needs and their children's needs, but they also began to care for men. The surplus that was created became the property of men. Because the men were mobile, (they had no *natural* relation to raising children) the surplus became theirs to trade with. They moved outside their local social units to other social units and they exercised control over trading and the market place.

Engles' study, *Origin of the Family*, which is inaccurate in terms of the origins of women's oppression is good once he establishes that women are oppressed. He equates women's oppression with the rise of class society. He never really says why people start having private property instead of communal property, only that women are oppressed and class society begins. Class society arose because of the oppression of women. With the surplus women created men could compete with other men who were similarly exploiting the surplus of their women. So, competing classes of men developed. They engaged in warfare, and ripped off other men's surplus, and came back to add it onto their own. They began to build an economic power base which was made possible by the original surplus value that women created. In other words, women's work made possible a class society in which some men could make

51

other men work for them. The exploitation of all women by all men made possible the exploitation of some men by other men.

The more exploitative the relationship between men and women becomes, the stronger and more vital become the institutions of male supremacy. So that in an advanced industrial society, men maintain their daily lives not at all. Male consciousness is largely determined by this fact. Male Marxist intellectuals who talk about production as the basis of consciousness and the primary material condition in people's lives are operating in a context that whatever is produced and reproduced in daily life is taken for granted. By whom it is done or how it is done is never questioned.

It would have been much more difficult for men to start and perpetuate class society if they got pregnant, gave birth, raised and maintained children and themselves. Their lives would have been dominated (as were women's) by raising food, playing with and supervising children, cooking, cleaning, building huts, making utensils, etc. Since they didn't have those responsibilities, didn't have to be there every day to keep the home running smoothly, didn't have to birth children so that there would even *be* a society, they could go off and start wars, stealing the surplus other men had expropriated and enslaving other villages.

Class Relation of Women to Men

In classical Marxist terms the relationship of wife to husband is one of slavery, as Hodee Edwards described:

"For, when a man is hired to work, the labor power he sells is a commodity he owns but did not produce: it was produced by labor power for which no payment is given. In all other cases, such a condition is called slavery. The man owns the 'means of production' of his commodity, namely, the woman. She, in performing her housework, produces the commodity he then sells and is paid for."[1]

The woman engages in certain material production and in return receives room and board. The degree to which she receives room and board is dependent on the kind of heterosexual privilege she has. If she has a heterosexual relationship with a ruling class man her return for the work she does is on a totally different level than if she has a heterosexual relationship with a working-class man or a pimp, whose access to the class structure is on the other end. Of course with divorce laws, changes in marriage laws, the right of access to their own earnings, the really feudal characteristics of that slave relationship have been somewhat modified. However, such laws are only an escape valve and function to maintain the family.

In case you don't think that the status of a wife is classically that of a slave, look at the facts. By law a woman is required to provide her husband with sexual relations and domestic services and she is required to follow his domicile. She has to acquiesce to sexual intercourse anytime he so desires: "A husband cannot be guilty of raping his own wife by forcing her to have sexual intercourse with him. By definition, the crime [of rape] is ordinarily that of forcing intercourse on someone other than the wife of the person accused."[2] She has to maintain his home (clean, cook, wash, mend, buy food, etc.), provide for his personal needs, and birth and take care of his children. Moreover, she has to live where he lives; if she refuses, she can be charged with desertion. Now *that* is the classic definition of a slave. A slave is the property of the owner. A slave's freedom of movement is curtailed. The owner is entitled to obedience and the time, labor and services of the slave.

53

In return the owner has only to feed, clothe, and house the slave, and not even adequately.

Such is a wife. In return for bed and board, she provides sexual services, reproductive ability (a woman has to have her husband's written consent to get her tubes tied) and domestic labor. Courts have ruled that the husband is legally entitled to his wife's domestic services and further that she *cannot be paid* for her work.[3] The husband--and through him all males--receives all her labor for subsistence only. She receives no wages directly; she is outside of the wage economy. Her work is unpaid, but absolutely socially necessary. Her domestic and sexual services make her husband's work possible and via each woman *all* male work possible. Her reproduction of the next generation gives her husband heirs and bosses future workers. As Betsy Warrior described it:

"Women are not just laborers in the male-defined sense of the word. Women are the source of all labor in that they are the producers of all laborers. This is the basic means of production (reproduction) in any society. It creates the first commodity, female and male laborers, who in turn create all other commodities and products. Men as the ruling class profit from this commodity through its labor. These profits come in two sizes: king-size and super. The individual man who is king of his castle (the patrilineal family) has his labor power produced, prepared, and maintained for him free. When he sells his labor power on the market he is selling a commodity he owns but did not produce, thereby profiting from the slave labor that went into the making of this product. The *male* capitalist class makes a super-profit when it buys this labor power and then receives the surplus value of its "outside" economy production."[4]

Of course, there are married women who do not do their own housework. The work they perform for their husbands is to have sex and reproduce children. These women are managers--the petit-bourgeoise of the class of women. Their heterosexual privilege gives them access to a class position which is high enough to hire someone else to do their work. Their husbands sub-contract through them and they get from their husband the resources to pay that someone else. Their class position is fundamentally different from the woman who is doing that work herself because their relationship to the creation of surplus value within the home is different. Either they are married to and perform sexual labor for a high class male or they have money through inheritance, access to their father's money. Whether married or not, it's the same heterosexual framework that allows them access to money.

It is important to note that there is a relation between the accumulation of capital in advanced industrial societies and primitive accumulation. In order for there to be advanced industrial societies, there have to be societies engaged in very low levels of primitive accumulation which the advanced society exploits. The same relationship exists between men and women. You have one whole segment of the population which does a certain kind of work which creates surplus value which another segment of the population takes over and uses. For the structure of capitalist society itself, the unpaid labor of the housewife is crucial. Unpaid labor in general is crucial to the ability of an economy to accumulate capital. The main reason that the U.S. is the richest industrial nation in the world is that for 200 years we had a slave population which received room and board for 200 years of labor. Some industrial societies had colonies and derived similar benefits by directly exploiting another population; we not only had colonies, we had a population within our own industrial structure which was totally slave. When you have a slave population you make a quantuum leap in what capital you can accumulate--a whole lot of money becomes capital that doesn't if it has to go back into wages or social services.

Role of Ideology

Within the women's movement there have been trends which indicate a lack of attention to the importance of the role of ideology. Ideology itself is a material force in history. It is not simply part of a super-structure defined by the productive base. Ideology is a world-view; it provides a way for us to perceive the world, to understand and incorporate what exists around us. Our perceptions of our environment are not simply reflections of what is out there. Our perception of a tree and what it is, is defined by how we have learned to understand trees. If we have a world-view in which plants are kindred spirits with whose continued life our life is inextricably bound, we will see a tree very differently than if we have a world-view in which nature is alien and has to be conquered or it will conquer us. The tree in either case is the same, it is the world-view, the ideology, that makes the difference.

The ideological assumptions functioning at a particular time determine the limitations within which people understand the so-called objective conditions around them. Not understanding this leads to economist trends--the leaflet mentality. Radicals hand out millions of leaflets explaining to people the *real* conditions of their lives. If they can just describe it right this time, the people will see and become revolutionaries. Passive receptor people plus right information equals revolution. What this leaves out is the ideological framework within which people's consciousnesses are formed. That framework of expectations, self-understandings, etc. creates the limits within which people can hear what you're saying.

The economist trend coupled with the Marxist mistake of trying to make working women fit into the male proletarian scheme has led to a lot of nonsense. Women are in the wage economy at various points because capitalism needs them, or because they're driven to get more money to feed their kids, not because they are no longer slaves. Working outside the home doesn't make women proletarian as long as their basic reproductive unit still puts them in a slave position. Their consciousness is still defined by the fact that they're slaves in the family, although it is complicated by the fact that they're also shit-workers in the wage economy.

Heterosexual Ideology

Ideological hegemony means that there is an ideology that exercises total control over the assumptions under which people live. Bourgeois ideology defines life by the hourly wage and that assumption permeates all consciousness. In order to get outside of that, in order to assume that something else ought to be the definition of work, there has to be a total critique of the assumptions upon which wage labor rests. The framework of understanding is the ideology; it acts as an active force in determining how you understand the situation around you, whether you see your situation as exploitation or a low wage. The ideology tells us what is *natural*. Bourgeois ideology tells us that there have always been bosses and workers, that it is natural that some work and some make decisions--that having your labor exploited by another is the natural order of things.

In terms of the oppression of women, heterosexuality is the ideology of male supremacy. In order for men to have a justification for exploiting women and an ability to enforce that exploitation, heterosexuality has to become, not merely an act in relation to impregnation, but the dominant ideology. Women must become defined as appendages to men so that there is a coherent ideological framework which says it is natural for women to create the surplus to take care of men and that men will do other things. Reproduction itself did not have to determine that. The fact that male supremacy developed the way it has and was institutionalized is an ideological creation. The ideology of heterosexuality, not the simple act of intercourse, is the whole set of assumptions and beliefs which maintains the ideological power of men over women. It is the basic framework which determines a woman's life from the earliest moments she learns to perceive the world. It tells her what is natural that she do and be.

Heterosexual hegemony insures that people think it natural that male and female form a life-long sexual/reproductive unit with the female belonging to the male. Male and female belong together, fit together, are basic to nature together. The purpose of life is to mate and have children, your *own* children. Now you go and tell people that there could be another purpose to life, that sexuality can be totally divorced from reproduction, that reproduction could be organized in a totally different way and they'll just laugh and say you're talking about Martians. Heterosexual hegemony insures that people can't even perceive that there could be other possibilities.

What is the position of lesbianism in the material conditions described above? The three factors that have to be considered are the relation of lesbians to production, reproduction and sexuality. At this point in history the primary role that lesbians have to play in the development of revolutionary consciousness is ideological.

Lesbians are objectively outside of the reality which heterosexual ideology explains. Therefore, they have the potential for developing an alternative ideology, not limited by heterosexuality. Now it is incredibly difficult to create and maintain that space. You can look at the parallel with bourgeois ideology. Bourgeois ideology has the power of every institution of society to maintain and enforce itself in the consciousnesses of the masses of the people. At moments of real crisis, people develop some resistance to bourgeois ideology, but whether they develop a real alternate ideology and conceive of things from a perspective that makes for revolution is another matter. You cannot criticize one little element of the ideology--like that wage isn't enough (trade-union consciousness)--you have to step outside of the whole ideology. Otherwise bourgeois ideology can accommodate that critique in a way that leaves all of its assumptions unquestioned. You have to find a way to critique those assumptions.

To continually question the assumptions of heterosexual ideology which has existed far longer than bourgeois ideology is just that much more difficult. You have to create the space that stands outside of all the assumptions of heterosexuality--assumptions about the family, about marriage, about motherhood, about housework, about childrearing, about rape, about illegitimacy, about spinsterhood--about everything that has to do with the relationships between men and women. To stand outside of heterosexual ideology and to develop an alternative way that male-female relationships could exist is an incredibly creative act. Revolutionary ideology posits new ways of understanding objective conditions, new goals; it posits what you want your future life to be. You make an ideology that says this is what it's going to look like and then you create it.

This doesn't mean that lesbians have their assumptions together. <u>It means that lesbians have a basis for creating new ways of understanding the material conditions. That is because lesbians stand in a different relation to the three material conditions that determine the class position of women--reproduction, production (domestic labor) and sexuality.</u> The lesbian does not have a domestic base that is defined by the production of new labor power and maintenance of her husband's labor power. Her primary relationship to class society is in proletarian terms. That element of slave consciousness which is integral to heterosexual women is missing. Her ability to understand the conditions of proletarian oppression is far greater. She does not have to work through the series of contradictions created by being in the slave position before she can relate to the fact that she's a proletariat in advanced capitalism.

What is the relationship between a new consciousness and an old consciousness? What is lesbian consciousness and what is heterosexual consciousness? Many lesbians in the lesbian movement talk and feel as if our strategy is to wait until all women become lesbians. The question, I think, is rather how all women will understand themselves. If the ideology of heterosexuality can be attacked and exposed and an alternative ideology can be developed, I'm not sure how important it is that all women stop being heterosexual. Because the way a woman would understand what it would mean to be heterosexual would be totally different. A critique of heterosexual ideology ultimately reduces heterosexuality to an act at the moment of impregnation. If you're going to have a baby, there is a role for heterosexuality. If we develop other ways to have babies, then what heterosexuality is becomes irrelevant.

Male supremacy is what is attacked in lesbian ideology. What we are doing in revolutionary struggle is to make our consciousnesses different. When enough people's consciousnesses are different, then we make a revolution. Changes in consciousness involve struggle; you don't just get presented with ideas and they change your consciousness. Struggle (action) makes apparent the contradictions between the new world-view and the reality we perceive. The tension between what we have come to understand as what we want and what is going on has to become clear. If we don't question the ideology, then the contradictions are not perceivable. It's very difficult to create that space without a total ideological struggle, which demystifies talk about cultural revolution versus material condition revolution. The revolutionary process itself involves a transformation in people. If that transformation doesn't occur, there will be no revolution.

[1] Hodee Edwards, "Housework and Exploitation: a Marxist Analysis," *The First Revolution: A Journal of Female Liberation* (Cambridge: Cell 16, 1971), p. 92.

[2] Court case cited by Sheila Cronan, "Marriage," *Notes from the Third Year: Women's Liberation,* (1971), p. 63.

[3] Court case cited by Sheila Cronan, "Marriage," *Notes from the Third Year: Women's Liberation,* (1971), p. 63.

[4] Betsy Warrior, "Slavery or Labor of Love," *The First Revolution: A Journal of Female Liberation* (Cambridge: Cell 16, 1971), p. 39.

LIVING WITH OTHER WOMEN

Rita Mae Brown

It is the primacy of women relating to women, of women creating a new consciousness of and with each other which is at the heart of women's liberation, and the basis for the cultural revolution. Together we must find, reinforce and validate our authentic selves. As we do this, we confirm in each other that struggling incipient sense of pride and strength, the divisive barriers begin to melt, we feel this growing solidarity with our sisters. We see ourselves as prime, find our centers inside of ourselves. We find receding the sense of alienation, of being cut off, of being behind a locked window, of being unable to get out what we know is inside. We feel a real-ness, feel at last we are coinciding with ourselves. With that real self, with that consciousness, we begin a revolution to end the imposition of all coercive identifications, and to achieve maximum autonomy in human expression.

from The Woman-Identified-Woman

Before the dawn of the woman-identified woman, back in the Age of Spermatic Oppression, women did love and live with other women. Two women met, fell in love, mar-

"Living With Other Women" appeared in *Women: A Journal of Liberation*, vol. II, no. 2.

ried and lived ever after. The women were forced to lead a double life if they were to economically and socially survive. It was a high price to pay but countless women paid it and are paying it still because life with another woman allows greater freedom for self-knowledge and far more emotional support. This kind of life, which I will call old gay, is another version of that great Amerikan lie, the Individual Solution. The Individual Solution means that you and your lover can stay aloof from the problems of others, work hard, save your money, budget wisely and lead the "good life". Lesbians had no choice in staying away from the problems of other people, they were never welcome. For old gay women the Individual Solution was the only road available to them. Along with the lie of the Individual Solution hung the albatross of love oppression. Women of the pre-woman-identified woman era were love drugged. Love was the answer. It solved all problems and if allowed to flow free it could solve the problems of the world. All a woman had to do was find that four letter word, love, and that other four letter word, life, just opened up and bloomed with eternal joy. Of course, you had to work to make love work--it was your life's work. Old gay women were just as oppressed by the love definition applied to women as heterosexual women because the definition makes women into a function (lover, comforter, companion) rather than a person. Since women were neither seen nor treated as persons, as full-fledged individuals, few women had a sense of self but only a sense of function.

Lesbians, although more independent by virtue of being free from a man, had internalized along with love oppression many other values of the establishment, and these were reflected in how they lived. For instance, old gay, like other forms of oppression, imitated the values of the dominant culture (the white, rich, heterosexual male) with few improvements. Class and race lines were more fluid but the standard was that of materialism and status within the system. In other words, you could move "up" much more easily in the old gay world than in the straight world but the values were much the same. Women who were married set up house together. Women who were unattached continued to look for someone to love and marry. It was all conducted underground so there was a taste of excitement to it and if you lived in one of the big cities, a taste of glamor. But it was the same pattern as the rest of society where you isolate yourself from others who share your oppression and try to "make it" on your own or in tandem.

Before the Women's Liberation Movement, old gay lesbians had organized into the Daughters of Bilitis. This nationwide organization did not and does not have radical politics. Its purpose was to promote greater understanding of the lesbian way of life, and hopefully, to allow lesbians to participate in the mainstream of society. In the late 1960's as Women's Liberation began to gather strength many old gay women became interested in the movement but remained outside it because of the theme of this issue: How we live and with whom. Old gay women knew from bitter experience that heterosexual women neither understood the lesbian living situation nor desired to understand it. The heterosexual women had accepted the male definition of women to such an extent that the idea of a woman living with and loving another woman was too threatening even though there was similarity in how they both lived. The early movement blatantly discriminated against the lesbian, in some cases expelling women who were lesbians. A few women refused to be repulsed. At the same time other old gay women helped found and shape the Gay

Liberation Movement. As the lesbians in Women's Liberation became increasingly dissatisfied over their treatment
at the hands of heterosexual women, the lesbians in Gay
Liberation became dissatisfied with their treatment at the
hands of homosexual men. These women came together
and tried to define what had been their lives and what
their lives were now becoming due to some heavy changes
in consciousness. Their effort became the paper, *The
Woman-Identified Woman.*

Woman-Identified Woman moved beyond the definition
of old gay and the traditional definition of women toward
a concept of women defining themselves. It sounds so simple and it is; yet, women are just beginning to define
themselves. A woman-identified woman is one who defines
herself in relationship to other women and most importantly as a self apart and distinct from other selves, not
with function as the center of self, but being. In other
words, only you can identify yourself; only you know who
you are. As long as you accept male values you cannot
accept yourself. The entire Women's Liberation Movement
has proved time and time again that those values never
granted woman a self, only a service. A woman can best
find out who she is with other women, not with just one
other woman but with other women, who are also struggling to free themselves from an alien and destructive culture. It is this new concept, that of woman-identified
woman, that sounds the death knell for the male culture
and calls for a new culture where cooperation, life and love
are the guiding forces of organization rather than competi-
tion, power and bloodshed. This concept will change the
way we live and who we live with.

The women who wrote *Woman-Identified Woman* and
the women who have come to understand it are in a transi-

tion period. We must move out of our old living patterns and into new ones. Those of us who believe in this concept must begin to build collectives where women are committed to other women on all levels--emotional, physical, economic and political. Monogamy can be cast aside, no one will "belong" to another. Instead of being shut off from each other in overpriced cubicles we can be together, sharing the shitwork as well as the highs. Together we can go through the pain and liberation of curing the diseases we have all contracted in the world of male dominance, imperialism and death. Women-identified collectives are nothing less than the next step towards a Women's Revolution.

None of us are there yet. Few of us are even in collectives much less woman-identified collectives. But at least we know what has to be done. This time of transition is a time of reaching out in the dark and hoping another sister's hand will reach back and connect. Knowing what has to be done makes it harder in some ways as we are more impatient for the collectives to materialize. It can be a time of anguish because we may be ready to try to build a woman-identified collective and find that no one else is ready to build with us. A collective, like a revolution, cannot be built by one woman. But it will come to pass. And when it does we will look back on our various lives as some old discarded rocket boosters and fully realize just how much we were compromised and strung out by a very basic matter: How we live and with whom.

THE SHAPE OF THINGS TO COME

Rita Mae Brown

If you love women then you are in revolt against male supremacy. The world which men have built hates women. Women, according to male supremacy, exist to serve the male. A woman who loves women then defies the basic building block of male supremacy: woman hatred. Women who love women are Lesbians. Men, because they can only think of women in sexual terms, define Lesbian as sex between women. However, Lesbians know that it is far more than that, it is a different way of life. It is a life determined by a woman for her own benefit and the benefit of other women. It is a life that draws its strength, support and direction from women. About two years ago this concept was given the name woman-identified woman. That's not a bad name, it is just a fancy way of saying that

Written on behalf of *The Furies*, "The Shape of Things To Come" appeared in *Women: A Journal of Liberation*, vol. II, no. 4.

you love yourself and other women. You refuse to limit yourself by the male definitions of women. You free yourself from male concepts of "feminine" behavior.

Lesbianism, politically organized, is the greatest threat that exists to male supremacy. How can men remain supreme, how can they oppress women if women reject them and fight the entire world men have built to contain us? The beginning rejection is to put women first in your life, put yourself first. If you do that then you begin to understand that the only way you can lead the life you would like to lead is by smashing male supremacy--and its offshoot oppressions, class and race supremacy.

Any oppressed person who gives in to her oppression insures that others will remain oppressed and she exposes her sisters who are fighting that oppression. The emerging political Lesbians, or women-identified women, realize the scope of male supremacy and are changing their lives to fight it. Women who remain silent leave these outspoken women to face the common oppressor. Committing yourself to women is the first concrete step toward ending that common oppression. If you cannot find it in yourself to love another woman, and that includes physical love, then how can you truly say you care about women's liberation? If you don't feel other women are worthy of your total commitment--love, energy, sex, all of it--then aren't you saying that women aren't worth fighting for? If you reserve those "special" commitments for men then you are telling other women they aren't worth those commitments, they aren't important. You also don't understand or else avoid recognizing that individual relationships--your "personal" life--is political. Relationships between men and women involve power, dominance, role play and oppression. A man has the entire system of male privilege to back

70

him up. Another woman has nothing but her own self. Which relationship is better for you? It's obvious.

If women still give primary commitment and energy to the oppressors how can we build a strong movement to free ourselves? Did the Chinese love and support the capitalists? Do the Viet Cong cook supper for the Yankees? Are Blacks supposed to disperse their communities and each live in a white home? The answer, again, is obvious. Only if women give their time to women, to a women's movement, will they be free. You do not free yourself by polishing your chains, yet that is what heterosexual women do.

Lesbians who have tried to pull women into a supportive women's community are often attacked by these heterosexual women who hang onto the privileges they get from their men. These Lesbian-haters are not always vicious women. Most of them don't understand how heterosexuality maintains male supremacy. They also don't want to understand because if they did then they would have to change their lives and lose the scant privileges men have given them. The facts are simple: Heterosexuality keeps women separated from each other. Heterosexuality ties each woman to a man. Heterosexuality exhausts women because they struggle with their man--to get him to stop oppressing them--leaving them little energy for anything else. For this destruction of women's communities, for this betrayal of other women, women indeed get privileges from men: legitimacy (you are a real woman if you are with a man--a sexual definition again), prestige, money, social acceptance, and in some token cases political acceptance.

If you are a Lesbian who has come out then you cut yourself off from those privileges. You have ended your stake in maintaining the heterosexual world. You are in total revolt against male supremacy. How can women liberate themselves if they are still tied to that male supremacist world? How can a woman tied to men through heterosexuality keep from betraying her sisters. When push comes to shove, she will choose her man over other women; heterosexuality demands that she make that choice. How can you build a serious political movement when women do this to each other? You can't. Lesbianism is a necessary step in the struggle for liberation.

Why would any heterosexual woman give up the privileges men grant her for being heterosexual? Most often she will only give them up if she sees there is something better than the crumbs thrown to her from men. What can Lesbianism offer? It offers double oppression. It offers the threat of getting fired from your job, estranged from your family and old straight friends, it offers getting your throat slit by straight women in the service of men, it offers constant struggle against an inhumane and diseased world where violence is the key to power and love is a word found in poetry but not on the streets. Why take on those burdens?

Because Lesbianism also offers you the freedom to be yourself. It offers you potential equal relationships with your sisters. It offers escape from the silly, stupid, harmful games that men and women play, having the nerve to call them "relationships." It offers change. You will change yourself by discovering your woman-identified self, by discovering other women. No one, not even another Lesbian, can tell you who that self is. It is your individual challenge, your life. You will be on unfamiliar ground with no old patterns to guide you. As you change yourself you will begin to change your society also. A free, strong self cannot live in the muck that men have made. You will make mistakes and suffer from them. You will hurt and be hurt trying to find new ways. But you will learn and push on. You will discover the thousand subtle ways that heterosexuality destroyed your true power; you will discover how male supremacy destroys all women and eventually the creators of it, men. You will find once your consciousness is raised it cannot be unraised. Once you have a vision of the new world you can no longer accept the old one. You will become a fighter. You will find love and that you are beautiful, strong and that you care. You will build communities with other women from all classes and races, those communities will change the material parts of our lives. You will share what you have with others and they with you. You will revolt against this whole filthy world that tried to cover you and your beauty under a ton of male supremacist slime. That is what Lesbianism offers you.

Those of us who have found those new lives, that hope and courage, find ourselves in the position of being attacked and undermined by women in the women's liberation movement to say nothing of forces outside that movement. We cannot allow ourselves to be oppressed by men; how then can we turn around and allow ourselves to be oppressed and harrased by women clinging to heterosexual privilege? We can't. Therefore, large portions of the political Lesbian population in women's liberation and gay liberation have split from those movements in order to survive. Does that mean we hate straight women? No. But would you volunteer your neck for someone to step on? Does this mean we can never again work with straight women or with gay men? No. But we aren't going to work with anyone until they begin

73

to change their behavior. Some changes are: they can no longer push us around, hide us under rugs or try to seduce us when everyone else has gone home only to deny us in the morning.

Straight women by virtue of being tied to men don't understand Lesbians or the political meaning of Lesbianism. Straight women don't know what our lives are like. They can't think like we do. We understand their lives because we were all raised to be straight. It is one-way communication. Straight women are confused by men, don't put women first, they betray Lesbians and in its deepest form, they betray their own selves. You can't build a strong movement if your sisters are out there fucking with the oppressor.

Further, as long as men have women under their control, they aren't going to change. By withdrawing support, men have to change. Sure a few individual men here and there will and have changed. Those few treat you and other women like human beings, but those men still haven't joined in the organized battle against sexism. They have to throw in their lot with us like any group dedicated to political change. Straight women are constantly bought off by the good behavior of a few rare men. Good behavior is not enough, he must join the struggle and take risks like the rest of us. Until that time, no man is our brother, he is still our oppressor. We can't work with straight women while they are misled by "good" men.

A short note about bisexuality. You can't have your cake and eat it too. You can't be tied to male privilege with the right hand while clutching to your sister with the left. Lesbianism is the only road toward removing yourself from male ways and beginning to learn equality.

Equality teaches strong lessons. Once you feel your

strength you cannot bear the thought of anyone else being beaten down. All other oppressions constructed by men become horrible to you, if they aren't already. Class and race, those latter day diseases sprung from sexism, maim and destroy people every bit as much as sexism itself. No oppression is tolerable. All must be destroyed. Once you have come out you can no longer fall back on race and class privilege, if you have any. Those privileges divide you from your Lesbian sisters who don't have them. Any Lesbian who tries to salvage her racial and class privileges does so at the expense of other Lesbians; she weakens all of us by this mistake. A mistake in recognizing the hatred of male supremacy for Lesbians, also; men award privilege for serving them--the Lesbian does not serve them, so you will be clinging to your privilege without really having the power to back it up. All you have left is the behavioral patterns born of those privileges, the bark without the bite--but that bark turns away other Lesbians. You don't automatically stop acting in those ways. In most cases you have to be taught by your Lesbian sisters who lacked those privileges and understand how divisive they are.

None of this is easy. Becoming a Lesbian does not make you instantly pure, perpetually happy and devotedly revolutionary. But once you have taken your life in your hands you will find you are no longer alone. There is a growing movement of Lesbians dedicated to our freedom, to your freedom, to ending all man-made oppressions. You will be part of that surge forward and you will leave your fingerprints on the shape of things to come.

The following is a very brief outline of practical program which is the first step toward organized struggle:

I. *Work Projects:* Women with economic privilege,

whether straight or Lesbian, Black, Asian, Indian, Latin, or White, should organize to meet the survival needs of women without economic privilege. This means food distribution centers, child care centers, health care centers, self-defense programs, skill centers and halfway houses.

II. Consciousness Raising: For all its abuses and misuse, consciousness raising still remains a good step toward understanding one's own oppression. If the C-R is disciplined, each woman should learn from other women and her own life, how those lives are a response to the dominant culture, the existing power structure. Women should learn that their personal lives reflect power politics on an individual level. By examining those lives and then going further to connect those lives into a pattern, women learn the mechanics of oppression. Once you know how something works you can fix it or fight it.

III. Media: We must develop and extend our own media--newspapers, films, magazines, art, music, etc. The existing white, male, rich media institutions distort the truth of any political movement and get rich off reporting our oppression in the bargain (e.g., David Susskind). It is imperative that we build our own media. No serious political movement in history has ever relied on the communications of its oppressor. Without our own media we are without voice.

IV. Ideology: Before we can advance as a political force, we must have a coherent, comprehensive ideology--a body of ideas that analyze our oppression in all its ramifications, economic, political, social, etc. A body of ideas that constructs the way to end that oppression. Lesbianism is the cornerstone for this structure. It is the touchstone of our independence, self-image, creativity. It is the distillation of women's oppression and the crystallization of women's power. Without this as our intellectual base we are doomed to reformism and disunity.

V. Organization: These last few years have seen work projects, C-R, the beginnings of media and the beginnings of clear ideology spring up throughout the country. All these activities are progressing at different rates of speed, different levels of understanding. If we are to forge a powerful political instrument to end our oppression then these activities must be co-ordinated toward that common purpose. This means that we must be organized, we must be a party. We must concentrate our forces rather than scatter them. The embryo of this concept, of organized struggle, is slowly growing. Lesbians are realizing that there will be no real political change without a party. Within five years we will have our party. With the formation of that body we will begin the second phase of our struggle against over 10,000 years of servitude. Forward, sisters, forward.

THE NORMATIVE STATUS OF HETEROSEXUALITY

The Purple September Staff

The following article was sent to us from a group of Lesbian/feminists from Holland who put out a newspaper called *Purple September.* We are printing the article because we feel that it furthers the discussion: Lesbianism is a Political Choice.

To many, feminism and lesbianism are two separate things that have little to do with each other. Feminism, they say, struggles against the oppression of all women and so its ranks are open to all women, straight or gay. What the feminist movement needs is solidarity among women regardless of the sexual and emotional preference of individual feminists.

An attractive line of thought, to be sure, but also one that overlooks a few things. To struggle against oppression --and to decide what is and what is not relevant in that struggle--you must first know what it is and how it occurs. You must know what the monster looks like, where it rears its ugly head and how it stays alive. All we can be sure of so far is that the inferior status of our sex continues to be reinforced in a great many different ways. The monster has many faces. We have been staring at one of them in particular over the last few years. Its name is female conditioning. The process known as consciousness raising has made women of all ages and every class aware of their childhood conditioning toward 'feminine' behavior, and of the catastrophic effects of that conditioning in their adult lives. As we grew up 'femininity' was defined for us in all sorts of ways, some explicit ('girls don't play football'), some implicit. One of the implicit definitions of 'femininity' was heterosexuality.--'You just wait until you have a boyfriend.'--All parents view their daughters as future lovers of men; few realize that this is where conditioning begins. For parents not only cherish the thought that their little girl will grow into a normal woman, they also make sure she does.

Now, oddly enough our heterosexual conditioning seems to be systematically barred from feminist analyses of women's oppression. I can think of only one explanation for this, and that is that boys are conditioned toward heterosexuality as well as girls. A 'real' man is a straight man, a 'real' woman is a straight woman. A gay fellow is effeminate, a gay woman, masculine. The straight norm applies to both sexes and thus does not count as part of the female conditioning as such.

Or so it seems, perhaps, to some, though not to me. The

overall objective of female conditioning is to make women perceive themselves and their lives through male eyes and so to secure their unquestioning acceptance of a male-defined and male-derived existence. The overall objective of male conditioning is to make men perceive themselves and their lives through their own eyes and so to prepare them for an existence in and on their own terms. The combined effect of both ways of conditioning is, therefore, the perpetuation of a power relationship between the sexes. The fact that both sexes are exposed to straight conditioning does not prevent the *concept* of heterosexuality from being linked, in male and female conditioning respectively, to opposite things that have opposite meanings. In male conditioning, male heterosexuality is linked to the male prerogative of a human identity; in female conditioning, female heterosexuality is linked to the denial of that same identity.

As long as feminism is out to abolish the existing power relationship between the sexes it cannot ignore the normative status of heterosexuality. Yet this is precisely what it has, so far at least, ignored. True, there are feminists who claim to be fully conscious of their conditioning in sexual as well as other terms. That they continue to be straight is, they say, a matter of personal preference. The trouble with this is that we live in a culture which sanctions only heterosexuality. As a result you cannot convince anyone that you are straight by choice. But that is not all. A personal decision in favor of heterosexuality is not the same as an analysis of its normative status. And feminists cannot go on pretending that such an analysis is not needed. This is true whether you are a feminist who claims to be straight by choice or one that regards her heterosexuality as fixed and unchangeable, a given as the color of her eyes. If it is a given in the life of one person, it has to be a given in the lives of all of us. And if that were so, no one would take the trouble to condition her children toward heterosexuality and culture could dispense with its taboos on, say, homosexuality. You may think that you could not be anything other than straight, but that does not alter either the normative status of heterosexuality or the need for a feminist analysis of that status.

Being gay as such does not determine your view of heterosexuality as a norm. If you are gay but have not come out, chances are you'd rather be straight. If you are gay and have come out, you may still consider yourself the victim of a cruel fate. If so, chances are you, too, would prefer to be straight. Rejecting straight relationships in your personal life is not the same as analyzing the norm that would make straight girls of us all. But as things stand now, not all the lavendar girls nor their straight sisters seem ready even to discuss it critically. Instead, they join hands in the struggle against the consequences of a norm which by tacit agreement is itself left undiscussed. As a result, gay women often are unable to ascribe to their own lesbianism a positive value that reaches beyond their personal lives. They cannot, that is, translate that value in feminist terms (nor integrate the two) because feminist terms are not personal. This is the gay counterpart of the impossibility of translating in feminist terms a personal decision in favor of heterosexuality. And so it turns out that from a feminist viewpoint it is indeed irrelevant whether feminists are straight or gay, but that is not the end of the story. Feminism does require that feminists *critically assess the normative status of heterosexuality* whether or not they abide by that norm in their personal lives.

The women of *Purple September* will take the bull by

the horns here and now, if you will pardon the expression. We reject the normative status of heterosexuality but not heterosexuality as one type of relationship among other, possible types. We do not doubt that there are straight relationships that derive their meaning and content from the people involved and not from the norm alone. But even in those relationships the male partner always has the option of falling back on 'masculine' behavior in the sense of his conditioning, thereby forcing his partner to fall back on 'feminine' acceptance in the sense of her conditioning. He has that option because the oppression of women by men has the status of a universal axiom: no one is surprised by 'axiomatic' behavior, but this is precisely how everyone confirms it. That is why the important thing is not that there are men who do not exercise the option they have. The important thing is that the option exists whether or not it is exercised.

The normative status of heterosexuality forces women to limit themselves sexually and emotionally to relationships with members of the caste that oppresses them, while denying them the possibility of establishing meaningful relationships with other women. Viewed in this light the straight norm is not really a sexual norm at all, but a powerful instrument in the perpetuation of the power relationship between the sexes.

Lesbianism can do nothing for the feminist cause as long as it is experienced and interpreted on the basis of tacit acceptance of the straight norm. For that reason we are not propagandists for the 'Greek way' (Lesbianism). But since we ourselves reject the straight norm we are able to experience our lesbianism as a (relative) given that integrates our feminism with our personal experience. Thus it is not lesbianism as such which is our choice, but its integrative function.

BISEXUALITY

Loretta Ulmschneider

Just as the existence of lesbians is not a new "phenomenon," so the existence of female bisexuals (women who relate sexually to both women and men) is not new. Many women have had lesbian relationships when young and then "reformed" themselves into heterosexuals, usually by getting married. These women obviously did not choose freely to be bisexuals. They either recognized their powerlessness without men, or bought the lie that they were "sick" and tried to "cure" themselves. Other women who were upper class, eccentric artists, actresses, etc. have had affairs with both women and men. Their bisexuality was often an indulgence granted by their men, or once again they used the men as a cover to gain social approval or as a means to more power and financial security.

Today some feminists are "choosing" bisexuality and

see this as a revolutionary act. I would like to analyze some of the ways this choice affects the personal lives of these women, the feminist movement, and male supremacy.

First, what does bisexuality mean as a personal choice for a woman? I do not intend to discuss all the nuances of the different stages women go through in order to recognize and define their own sexuality, i.e., the period when a woman is coming out. I do *not* question the merits of that process. But I do question why a woman eventually "chooses" to remain suspended in all the confusions and conflicts bisexual relations can create. One of these conflicts is the question of how she uses the strengths she gains from her woman lover. The lover often feels that her energies were used to regenerate the bisexual woman until she was able to deal with men again. Because of this and other conflicts, both women involved often feel that energies were dissipated completely.

Whether the bisexual woman loses energy from these conflicts or not, how does she become woman-identified? The relationships she still maintains with men do affect how she defines herself and judges her own self-worth. What the men demand and expect of her, how they react to her, what needs of theirs she meets or doesn't meet, their views of the world, etc., all influence how she views herself. Whether the influence is brutal or subtle, she is exposing herself to male sexism on all those levels. Perhaps she takes that risk because she believes men need to deal with their sexism. But why play that same old nurturing role women have always played for men? Why does she still define part of herself in terms of male needs. Though she has a woman lover, she is avoiding the risk of setting herself completely apart from male needs and dependence on men. She is losing the chance to build a new self around her own and other women's needs. To reclaim our bodies and ourselves is the most basic and necessary step to building a feminist revolution. Without a strong base in ourselves, our efforts to work together will be crippled.

Secondly, how does a female bisexual affect male supremacy? Because men still have their needs met by her, she supports rather than threatens male power. In return she receives most of the heterosexual privileges of a straight woman. She has access to whatever financial benefits and connections to power her man does. Even if his economic security is minimal, she still gains the social security that male approval gives you in this society. Her identity is much less likely to be questioned, and she therefore escapes both the insecurity of being manless in a man's world and the prejudice lesbians often face in obtaining and keeping jobs and housing.

The creation of a tolerant attitude toward bisexuality would actually be very advantageous for men. It would increase their sexual freedom without shaking their hold on power. It could easily become a double standard, in the same way that heterosexual promiscuity results in less punishment for men than it does for women. Just as long as men are the priority of women, men could allow women to have an occasional affair with a woman. In the privileged classes, it would be a reward just like a new dishwasher, house, maid, etc.

If a bisexual woman is only asking men to grant her some sexual freedoms, then she clearly does not have the same goals as feminists who intend to seize that power from men. If she does recognize feminism as a struggle for power, problems still arise. How does her feminism justify a diversion of primary energies to men? Because of the privileges she gains from men, and because she has not

87

made a clear choice and commitment for women, she invites the mistrust of feminists who have done so. What are her priorities? It is difficult and often debilitating to work with women whose commitments are not clear, and who cling to privileges without recognizing the power they gain from them.

Beyond the questions of woman-identity and the need for a high level of trust in small group situations, there is the question of ideology. If a bisexual woman does not see supremacy, how will she go on to analyze male power in deeper and broader ways, especailly heterosexuality as an institution that furthers male power. Does she see the need for an ideology? Will she participate in strategies which aim to destroy men's hold on power and therefore will also hurt the privileges she has gained from men?

Having looked at bisexuality within the context of the feminist struggle in a male supremacist society, let me end with this statement. As lesbian/feminists we affirm the bisexuality of human nature. This is one reason we refuse to beg for reforms as a minority group. We are not a minority. Lesbians represent that part of every woman that male supremacy has destroyed or suppressed. One goal of our revolution is to have a society where no particular expression of sexuality is enforced. *BUT*, the revolution has not happened yet. This is not utopia. Women who practice bisexuality today are simply leading highly privileged lives that do not challenge male power and that, in fact, undermine the feminist struggle. We are not trying to enforce lesbianism. We are asking women to look at how their lives affect male power and to make choices accordingly.

The Furies, March-April, 1973

COMING OUT IN THE WOMEN'S MOVEMENT

Coletta Reid

In the winter of 1969-70, I joined a consciousness raising group and a newly formed women's newspaper. My life had been typical of a well-socialized American female. I had interrupted college at twenty to marry a man both older and above me in social class. I supported him through graduate school, then went back to school myself to get a degree. I started graduate school, dropped out when my first child was an infant, returned to school then dropped out again. Finally, I got pregnant a second time because I didn't know what else to do.

Graduate school had been all too depressing. I never had a woman teacher; one teacher even boasted that he would refuse to teach in a department with a woman. Another upon meeting me suggested I do my thesis with him, after staring at my legs for five minutes. I had become unable to complete my work, an "erratic underachiever," they said. It was becoming clear that there were no teaching jobs available for women in my field; the possibilities of work were the same ones I had already been through: waitress, nurses' aide, secretary, admitting clerk in a hospital. My husband was angry at my long periods of depression and what he called "my low level of functioning"-- "I don't see why you can't have this apartment clean and dinner fixed when I get home. You have nothing else to do all day."

Thus at 27, pregnant and with a toddler, I came to the women's movement. I had never been in a political movement before. I tended toward the conservative end of liberalism, I suppose. After all, I *had* married "up", the system had been good to me. I was extremely naive about power. I remember clearly the first time I realized my husband wasn't in total sympathy with the movement. I brought home a newspaper account of women sitting-in at a male-only university karate course. He said that women only wanted to be violent like men. I asked whether defending yourself against rape was being violent like a man. He countered that rape was hardly a big enough reason to train yourself to become a potential killer. From then to the end only took nine months.

For the month before I asked him to leave, I had a recurring dream: I was a leaf in the wind being tossed and turned to and fro endlessly. To stop the dream I had to wake myself up. I realized that I had never really imagined myself without a man. I had always assumed I would get married. I had never *really* thought I would have to support myself and/or my children by myself all of my life. I was suddenly scared to death of the lack of structures in my life: no marriage, no family, no job, no reason to be living in the city I was in. (I had come there for my husband's job.) I now had to do everything for myself, make my own life choices, deal with the world myself. I found that I had no center to myself; my center had always been my husband, or my husband/children.

How had I come to such a frightening decision? Through working with women for the liberation of women. At first my husband became irrelevant; he wasn't nearly as exciting and provocative as the women I was working with. He had very little to say about my oppression; he wasn't interested in putting all his time and energy in on behalf of women. Later he became a hindrance; his needs had always come first in the marriage and to change that was a constant battle.

Almost everything I was reading at the time lead me toward lesbianism. If "The Myth of the Vaginal Orgasm" was true, then intercourse was not necessary or even relevant to *my* sexual satisfaction. If "Sexual Politics" was right that male sexuality was an expression of power and dominance, then I was choosing my own oppression to stay in a relationship with a man. If sex roles were an invention of society, then women--not just men--were possible people to love, in the fullest sense of that word. If I could hug and kiss a woman I loved, why couldn't I touch all of her body? Since my husband really thought men were superior, then wasn't my needing to be in a relationship with someone superior to me, self-hating and woman-hating? The conclusion seemed inescapable. I asked my husband to leave; he took our son and I kept our daughter.

Lesbian Oppression

Deciding that a course of action is best and carrying it out are two different cans of worms. I had some sense of the tremendous changes in my own psychology becoming a lesbian would require; I had no conception of the roadblocks society would throw up. Telling my family was my first shock; I said that I was getting divorced in order to become independent. My parents were furious; how could I break up my family for such a selfish and self-centered reason. I was just trying to shirk my responsibilities. I was lucky to have such a nice husband. He never beat me; he didn't drink; he didn't have a mistress; he supported me well. I was ungrateful; I didn't realize how lucky I was. My father yelled at my mother. She had failed in raising me. My mother blamed herself; she didn't understand where she had gone wrong. I clearly had become a "bad woman." My mother stopped being sympathetic; my father withdrew in hurt and anger. My mother said my father felt I had been mean to *him*. How? Because I had divorced Bob. Men stick together to the end.

That was only the beginning. I was getting my initiation into lesbian oppression. Most of the women I worked with were surprisingly non-committal. I had expected joy and jubilation, since I was choosing myself, other women, and strength. The non-committal attitude turned into outright hostility whenever I discussed the political implications of my choice. It might have been ok if I had said that my choice was purely personal, that it had no relevance to any other feminist's life. But to suggest that becoming a lesbian might be a happier, more whole way of life for any feminist was too much. In a newspaper article my politics were identified with those of Norman Mailer--sexual fascism: Mailer required all women to be heterosexual and I required them all to be lesbian. Of course, it was ignored that Mailer had every institution in society on his side making heterosexuality the only choice even imaginable to 90% of the women in America. To compare that to one woman's voice with no power behind it except perhaps a glimmer of truth was and is ludicrous.

The full range of attitudes and prejudices came out in the course of a meeting of a daycare center I had helped found and worked in for nine months. One woman expressed misgivings about me or my friends being around

94

her daughter since I had become a lesbian. She evidently thought I would molest her little precious; she had no similar qualms about my being around her son when I was heterosexual. Nor had she any qualms about the heterosexual men being around her daughter which is strange since 100% of the child molestation cases reported in D.C. last year were committed by men. Another woman said she thought lesbians were too hostile, angry and man-hating to be around children who needed love and good vibes. Someone expressed regret at my husband's leaving since he was one of the few men she could relate to. Better to have a man around to relate to than have a fellow sister grow and become strong. The sexism inherent in almost all the responses was glaring. Some of the men at the daycare center were outrageously piggy toward the children but they were never called on the carpet at a meeting or put in the position of having to defend themselves as I was. In general the parents agreed that they were open to their children becoming bi-sexual but they certainly didn't want them encouraged to become little dykes and faggots.

I slowly left the women's movement or more accurately I was slowly pushed out. I had never envisioned myself a lesbian/separatist when I left my husband. The women's movement had given me the ideas, strength and support to do something I thought best for me and womankind; I had no idea it would reject me once I had done it.

Heterosexual Privilege

I had heard the term "heterosexual privilege" before, but I never really understood how it worked. Now I knew. When I was heterosexual I was accepted as normal by my family, friends, acquaintances, and contacts. But once I started putting myself and other women *first* in my life I was variously seen as: unnatural, immoral, perverted, disgusting, sick or a sexual fascist. In general, heterosexual feminists felt themselves superior to lesbians since they were involved in natural relationships. If I was honest about my lesbian relationship, I was flagrant. When they met their men at the door with kisses, that was normal. They were willing to accept my lesbianism only if it was secreted and viewed as minor to my life. They kept telling me it didn't make any difference who I personally loved. But I knew it made a tremendous difference. I was beginning to get the feeling that lesbianism was of crucial importance to feminism. Otherwise, why was I being oppressed so much for it, why was it so threatening to both men and women.

As I tried to live as an open lesbian I began to see the privileges I had taken for granted when married. My husband had been able to make more money than my lover and I together. There were no daycare centers for children under three since, of course, mothers should stay home and let their husbands work. But my lover couldn't make enough money as a waitress to support us both. My husband had taken the car; I was unable to get a loan for another one. I had no credit as it was all in my husband's name. Landlords wanted to rent houses to families; I had to pretend I was straight to get a job.

I realized that when I was married I had been bought off. I had accepted being subservient, sexually available, and keeper of his home in return for some degree of economic security and social acceptance. I had become a fat hen who gave up her freedom for regular corn. Being a bird who could fly was risky; and you ended up not nearly as well-fed. At some point in my life I had sold out as a form of survival.

The saddest revelation was that feminists still had a stake in being fat hens. They primarily wanted the farmer to treat them a little better. My co-workers at the newspaper were threatened by my becoming a lesbian. If I could do it, they could do it. They could stop co-operating in their oppression. They could choose to be lesbians, lesbians weren't born, they were made. I wasn't a rich artist who lived in Paris, I was an ordinary housewife with two kids and no skills, who with the help of women's liberation had taken her life into her own hands. And they could too. Even in the women's movement, women punish other women who stop accepting their role as weak, passive and dependent. Women who step out of line are threatening because they offer that choice as a possibility to others.

Myths About Lesbians

Most women accept the male myths about lesbians without questioning the use of those myths to keep women apart. Lesbianism is threatening to male social power because it represents the spectre of women united in their own interests. It is threatening to individual male power because it represents the loss of a personal servant, plus an always available sperm receptacle. It is quite inconceivable to most men that women could actually prefer female company and bodies to their own. The male ego is closely linked to his sense of superiority over women; he is outraged to think a "mere" woman could be thought his equal.

The most common myth accepted was that lesbians wanted to be men; they were unhappy male egos trapped in female bodies; they had confused sexual identities.

In fact, lesbians don't even like men and the world they've made. Why would anyone want to be rapists, perpetrators of wars and sexual and racial oppression, pollutors and capitalists? Certainly no self-respecting woman. Lesbians do, however, want many of the freedoms men have reserved for themselves. They want self-determination over their own bodies and children. They want access to the many areas men have forbidden them: governing the society through decision-making at all levels, physical strength and athletic ability, knowledge and skills from plumbing to bio-chemistry. Lesbians see the whole world as their province and aren't content to be restricted to woman's place.

The second myth is that lesbians embody in exaggerated form all the despicable qualities of men. They are always "on the make," they rape women, molest children, and view other women as "sexual objects." In fact, men have taken those very qualities women fear them for and have projected them onto lesbians. Thus women end up fearing lesbians more than men. By making lesbians "bogeywomen" men have kept women from loving and respecting each other, thereby robbing us of our greatest strength and potential for unity.

The third most common myth is that lesbians are just as involved in role-playing as are heterosexual couples--everybody knows about butch and femme. The aim of roles is not simply to divide all behavior, dress, jobs, etc. into two separate spheres. The aim is to make one set the superior role, to give one role power over the other. When two women are involved in a relationship, neither of them has the real social power behind a role to fall back on. Even if there is a "butch," she cannot marshall social pressure of family, friends and acquaintances to keep her femme dependent. She can't legally rape her (in marriage there is no rape); she can't leave her with five kids and no job; she has no church, marriage contract, or legal structures on her side. Behind the male role is social power, economic clout and physical strength. There is no such reality behind a butch.

Lesbians, in fact, are women and as such, they have all been socialized to be women. Most are actively involved in trying to overcome that female-training; they want to be what straights call "butches." They want to be physically strong enough to defend themselves; they want to be psychologically able to put their own needs and growth first; they want skills and jobs so they can support themselves and take care of themselves and each other. They want to be women who can establish relationships with each other out of mutual love, respect and equality--not out of desperate need and economic necessity. Lesbians do not sit and passively wait for a female knight in shining armor to come take them away to bliss. They are not looking for a love partner whom they can take care of, live through, and dedicate their lives to, secure in a role. Together, they *are* engaged in a fight to build positive, active, aggressive selves who can take control of their lives.

One stereotype concerns lesbians wearing male clothing. Lesbians wear male clothing because it's more comfortable, better made, more durable, cheaper and doesn't immediately brand you as a potential "sex object" to all men. Female clothing, just like female hair styles, and "feminine mannerisms" are all aimed at making the differences between men and women readily apparent. If men and women dressed and acted alike only *very* large men and *very* small women would be easily recognizable. How would men know who to treat as inferior, who to hire as secretaries, who to rape? Female clothing keeps women less mobile and more physically vulnerable. Ever try to escape from or fight a rapist in tight baggies and stacked heels?

Lesbianism & The Feminist Analysis

When I left marriage and the family, I was uncertain about the connection between the liberation of women and lesbainism. I only knew that becoming a lesbian was tredously significant to my life. As I encountered the oppression that society heaps on lesbians I sensed that lesbianism must be, in some way, crucial to ending the exploitation of women.

The feminist analysis of women's condition asserts the exploitation of women as a *sex*--women are exploited by men because they are women, because they have different genitals. Women's biology dictates that new generations of people be produced via women's bodies; in other words women provide *necessary* social labor just by being women. Through the process of becoming impregnated, carrying a child, and giving birth, woman performs an absolutely socially necessary task. Men have taken this biological fact and turned it into an ideology about woman's place.

Because some women must give birth each generation, men have constructed an ideology which says that:

1) The aim of all women's lives is to give birth. (Motherhood)

2) Because vaginal intercourse is necessary to impregnation, all sexual activity must have vaginal intercourse as its end. (Heterosexuality)

3) Because male impregnation is necessary to birth, women must bind themselves for life to the man who impregnates them. (Marriage)

100

4) All women must not only birth but also raise children. Women have a necessary relation to providing for children's day-to-day needs. (The Family)

5) Because women take care of children and are married, they must also take care of their men, which they cannot do properly if they leave the home to work. If they leave the home to work, it must be for the preservation of the home and they must still meet their husband's and children's daily needs. (Housewifery)

6) If women work outside the home, it should only be in the capacity of meeting men's needs (waitresses, secretaries) or children's needs (teachers, nurses). Because it is less important than men's work (the primary work), it can be paid less. (Job discrimination)

Men have taken the natural fact that woman reproduces the species and constructed an ideology that says that motherhood, heterosexuality, marriage, the family, housewifery and a secondary place in the job market are natural. In early feminist analysis, all of those "natural" constructs were challenged except heterosexuality. Early feminism took for granted that "natural sexuality" was heterosexuality; that "natural sexual relations" was vaginal intercourse; that female sexuality must be directed toward men. In other words, feminists still felt themselves to be "naturally" dependent on men for sexual satisfaction.

Women's sexuality *per se* is in no way naturally or necessarily connected to penises or penile penetration. Fucking *once* is necessary to getting pregnant once, that's all. Female orgasm originates in the clitoris whose stimulation is only peripherally involved in intercourse. Many other forms of clitoral stimulation are more effective than penile interpenetration. In fact, the vagina's only function is as a passageway between the external organs of sensual satisfaction (clitoris, labia, plevic floor, etc.) and the reproductive organs (uterus, fallopian tubes, etc.). The vagina has sensory nerves only at its entrance. This is not to deny that the vagina contracts during orgasm, so does the uterus; but orgasm originates in the clitoris and is dependent on clitoral stimulation. So, although it's possible for women to experience orgasm during intercourse; intercourse isn't necessary or even the "best way" for women to achieve sexual satisfaction.

However, men seem to think that it is the best way for men to achieve sexual satisfaction. So they have used female sexuality in service of their own. They have placed their own sexual interests ahead of women's during the course of which they have totally distorted female sexuality: "Men need sex more than women; women are naturally masochistic (they get pleasure from pain); if women don't enjoy fucking, they're frigid; the only orgasm is vaginal; if women don't have orgasm during intercourse, it's their own fault, etc." Male sexuality then has become a matter of male imposition of his supposed sexual needs upon women, with a mythology developed to justify it.

In other words, heterosexuality as an institution operates for the benefit of men. It is in men's interests for women to think that they "need" men for sexual pleasure, to think that vaginal intercourse is the only "natural" expression of female sexuality. Heterosexuality keeps women thinking that without a man in their lives they have to become asexual. Women are taught that the only way to get physical affection and sexual satisfaction is to be heterosexual. Thus women have seemingly "chosen" heterosexuality--and generally think that women who haven't are a deviant minority.

In the context of the institutional nature of enforced heterosexuality, lesbianism is an act of individual rebellion. The lesbian refuses to make the male's sexual "needs" primary. She sets out to reclaim her own sexuality, discover her own sexual needs and aggressively pursue them with other like-minded women. Female sexual passivity is central to heterosexuality. Women wait for men to make a date, make the first move, and finally to "get it up." Men are "turned off" by women who are aggressive and pushy about what they want and need. It is no accident that the "missionary" position is the favored one in advanced patriarchy. The man is "on top" in bed just as he is in the economy and politics. The woman is pinned down, can hardly move, and has the least chance of having an orgasm. If marriage is legalized prostitution, then heterosexuality is socially approved rape.

Thinking that your sexuality has to be directed toward men is analagous to thinking that your life must be directed toward men. Both are part of an ideology aimed at making and keeping women dependent. If women continue to lend their bodies to men to be used and entered for male pleasure, they are going to find it very hard to keep from lending their lives to men to be used for their ends.

In a world devoid of male power and, therefore, sex roles, who you lived with, loved, slept with and were committed to would be irrelevant. All of us would be equal and have equal determination over the society and how it met our needs. Until this happens, how we use our sexuality and our bodies is just as relevant to our liberation as how we use our minds and time.

Bibliography

Amazon Expedition: a lesbianfeminist anthology, Phyllis Birkby, Bertha Harris, Jill Johnston, Esther Newton & Jane O'Wyatt, editors. Times Change Press, $1.75. An excellent anthology of ten essays including Ti-Grace Atkinson on lesbianism and feminism, Joanna Russ on man-hating, Bertha Harris on the 1920's Paris lesbians and Rebecca Patterson on Emily Dickinson.

Lesbian Nation: The Feminist Solution by Jill Johnston. Simon and Schuster, $2.95. Difficult stream-of-consciousness writing but the section "Lesbian Feminism" pp. 148-191 is a brilliant exposition of the sexual underpinnings of patriarchy.

Lesbians Speak Out, Judy Grahn, Wendy Cadden, Brenda Crider, Sunny, Jane Lawhon & Anne Leonard, editors. Women's Press Collective, $3.00. A wonderful collection of lesbian writings including poetry, photographs and drawings. "About 80 lesbians have a piece of their real selves in this collection" which makes it the most representative and wide-ranging record of lesbian experience and feeling to come from the gay women's movement.

Lesbian/Woman by Del Martin and Phyllis Lyon. Bantam, $1.50. A very thorough account of their experiences with a wide variety of lesbian women by the two founders of DOB. Originally rejected by McCall Publishing because the authors "apparently had no doubts about their life style."

Motive: lesbian/feminist issue, Joan Biren, Rita Mae Brown, Charlotte Bunch & Coletta Reid, editors. Motive magazine, $1.00. Articles, poetry and graphics collected in the early stages of the lesbian/feminist movement. Articles on lesbians and: motherhood, the male homosexual movement, coming out, class, and feminism. A good introductory work.

Sappho Was A Right-On Woman by Sidney Abbott and Barbara Love. Stein and Day, $1.95. An account from personal experience by two women who were lesbian/feminist activists in New York. Includes the story of lesbian oppression in N.Y. and national N.O.W. and a discussion of the historical connections between lesbianism and the women's movement.

All books can be ordered from the women's mail order houses: First Things First, P.O. Box 9041, Washington, D.C. 20003 or A Woman's Place, 5251 Broadway, Oakland, California 94618.